senior moments

Prayer-chats with God about aging joy-fully

Bernadette McCarver Snyder

AUTHOR OF *Senior Moments* AND *Aging—with a Laugh and a Prayer*

TWENTY-THIRD
PUBLICATIONS

TWENTY-THIRD PUBLICATIONS
1 Montauk Avenue, Suite 200, New London, CT 06320
(860) 437-3012 » (800) 321-0411 » www.twentythirdpublications.com

Cover photo: ©iStockphoto.com/ Michael Kempf

ISBN: 978-1-62785-211-1
Library of Congress Catalog Card Number: 2016909029
Printed in the U.S.A.

A Division of Bayard, Inc.

DEDICATION

*Happiness is a butterfly
which, when pursued,
is always just beyond your grasp,
but which, if you sit down quietly,
may alight upon you.*
NATHANIEL HAWTHORNE

*He who masters the gray
everyday is a hero.*
DOSTOYEVSKY

I dedicate this book to
all of the seniors who mutter
but master every gray day.

INTRODUCTION

I have learned that senior-itis has a lot of problem-itis but also plenty of blessings and discoveries and downright funny experiences. As I wend my way through the "golden" years, I have found that it may be painful when this bone does *not* connect with that bone the way it is supposed to do, but it may still be workable if I make every bone connect with my funny bone!

So one day when I was muttering to myself and laughing at my "senior moments," I got the crazy idea that I could maybe learn to "pray" by writing down some of the daze of my days. I knew I wasn't organized enough to really "journal" every day like some people do, but maybe I could jot down some of the wonderings and wanderings in my head and my house in a once-in-a-while, some-days way.

So I did that. And it became a book titled, *Senior Moments*.

But, as my friends will tell you, when I start telling stories I don't know when to stop, so I kept writing down *more* of my musings and mutterings and soon I had enough for another book—and this is it! I hope you like it.

Brown paper bags

Dear Lord, it's a loverly summer day today, so I need to go out into the sunshine. I will drive down to the farmers market where I will find fresh-picked corn and tomatoes and maybe a small bunch of home-grown posies or a basket of ripe peaches for a pie.

I know I can get all this at the supermarket, but it's just not the same. When I unload the kinda dusty brown bags of goodies in my kitchen, I feel like I just grew them and picked them by hand myself.

Lord, you know I am crazy like that. I also drag in odd little leftover goodies from garage sales and treasure them as though they once belonged to my great-grandmother. That's so much more fun for me than buying something new from the department store.

This is not a recent quirk to enjoy these things because they are old just like me. No, I've just always loved "shopping" this way, ever since I journeyed into the future and discovered tiny little unusual shops or neighborhood garage sales far and near.

Lord, I know the day will come when I can't jump in my car and go adventuring because I'll be too ancient to drive, but I'll worry about that tomorrow. Today I am following the sun, and who knows what treasures I might bring home to delight me and shock some of my more formal friends who have different tastes than mine.

I have to confess that sometimes I kinda enjoy shocking them! But I really treasure those friends and their difference—even more than I treasure my odd little leftover goodies. Different strokes for different folks makes life more fun!

Dear Lord, thank you for different faces and different places, different youngsters and different oldsters, different ways of thinking and different ways of praying and loving you.

A trashy day

Dear Lord, one of my best friends got thrown out of my house this morning. I knew one day it would come to this, and I had prepared for it. Many of my friends have had a similar experience so I knew they would share my sorrow when I had to throw my old beloved coffee pot into the trash can.

When I bought it, it was little and plain, not a fancy pot with all the bells and whistles; but it looked interesting to me, and besides, it was on sale. When I tried it the next morning, I just put in the coffee and the water, and in about sixty seconds I poured out a steaming delicious cup of coffee, which was just the right amount to get me going. But there's another reason I loved this pot: it had a personality. After I poured my coffee, the pot would suddenly cough and chug and blow out a blast of steam as if to say, "So there!"

I knew right away that this pot was sooo good it might not last long with all that letting off steam, so I hurried back to the sale and bought another identical pot and stashed it on a shelf in the garage. As it turned out, my special blaster lasted lots longer than I expected, but then one day it just blew out its last blast and quit. No more steamy tantrums, no warning sign—just quit. I was sad, but I was "prepared" for the loss; so this morning on the way back from the garbage can, I picked up the new pot in the garage, took it to the kitchen, plugged it in, and was happy to see that it too has little steamy tantrums.

Lord, sometimes I want to blow out a blast of steam and just quit too but I can't because I don't have a spare "me" in the garage. So I just simmer and mutter to myself.

As we get older, our treasures and our helpers age too, and we have to be prepared for losses; but we can still enjoy finding new small surprises that just "fit your fancy." It's the same way with people. You meet new people, and some come with bells and whistles and are a lot of fun. On the other hand, some are plain and unsocial, but they have secrets like the steamy tantrums and you just have to learn to love them for their quirky ways.

Well, I've got to go now, Lord, but thank you for coffee pots and interesting friends, for steamy cups of coffee to warm up my crotchety bones, and, especially, thanks, Lord, for giving us this time we have together.

Wobbly wanderings

Dear Lord, I called a friend this morning to check
to see how she was doing. She said, "Oh, I'm making it but I've been furniture walking today."
Furniture walking? I thought she must be feeling
great if she was going out to shop for new furniture.

"No, no," she said. "Did you never hear that
expression before?" No, no, I did not. So she explained that when a senior has a wobbly day he or
she gets around the house by using the furniture.
When you get out of a chair, you reach out to grab
onto whatever piece of furniture is nearest and
hang on to it. Then you take a couple of steps and
reach for the next piece of furniture—small table,
chair, desk, whatever. By wobbling along this way,
by hanging on to the furniture, you can move
through the house—to answer a doorbell, get to
the kitchen to fix a snack, or "travel" slowly, wherever you need to go.

My goodness! Maybe everybody is familiar with
this expression, but I had never heard it before.
On my wobbly days, I have often furniture walked
through my house and didn't know I was doing it.

Yes, some say I seldom know what I am doing, but that's OK. I still get wherever I need to be whenever I need to be there, if I have to travel by cane, car, land, sea, or furniture walking.

Dear Lord, you know that whenever I start to wobble, I usually reach out to grab onto you and hold on for dear life. Unlike the furniture, you are always just where I need you to be. You are just what I need to hang onto in order to wend my way through this strange forest of senior problems, worries, or wobbles.

Thank you, Lord, for your helping hand and for friends who often surprise me with a new expression or idea or helpful hint or a really funny new joke that helps me giggle as I wobble.

An expensive lesson

Dear Lord, I never thought changing a light bulb would cost me $50, but it did this week. The burned-out bulb was located in a very hard-to-reach area of the house, but when I used to be taller (!), I could climb up a ladder and not-too-easily replace it.

The problem is that this bulb is in a "decorative" container. It's in a fancy white china thing that looks like a chef's puffy white hat, and the hat is held on by two tiny screws that, if you dropped them, it would be impossible to ever find match-ables for them.

I sent out an SOS to my tall grandson, and he hurried in and immediately dropped one of the screws, which I managed to grab before it went down the drain. He then removed the china "hat," which I grabbed quickly and placed in a safe place. And then he replaced the old bulb with a brand-new one from a package that had not been opened. The light did not dawn.

The bulb was one of those scrawly new ones that I don't really trust, so I got out an unopened package of the old-time plain bulbs, and he put one in. The dawn did not come.

Oh no! I figured it must be a faulty switch, which meant I needed to call a handyman. I called, and he came and looked at the area and asked if he could take the bulb out that was burning brightly in the family room. What? I thought I must have called an *un*handyman, but he took the family-room bulb, screwed it in where the burned out one had been, and immediately the dawn came. He said, "I'm sorry. You just had two brand-new bulbs that didn't work. I should have told you to try an old one that was working before you called me, but I didn't think about it." And then he gave me his bill for the service call.

Dear Lord, I am going to call all my friends and share with them my lesson learned. I will warn them that even brand-new light bulbs, hermetically sealed in a clear covering, *can* go bad. And I will snicker when I remind them that sometimes an old bulb can burn even brighter than a new untried one. Hooray for seniority!

How to not *open sesame*

Dear Lord, by the sink in my bathroom, I have
two look-alike containers that must be opened by
squeezing lightly. One is a miracle cream that you
smooth on to look twenty years younger (?!!). The
other is my toothpaste. This morning I squeezed
one of the containers and lightly spread toothpaste
on my cheeks. Immediately a face alert went off,
and I quickly soaped off the toothpaste—but my
face smelled minty the rest of the day.

I do not need to list this as an aging problem,
because I have had many "what did you do now?"
events like this in my past. Like many seniors,
I have put the trash out on the wrong day, mis-
placed the car keys, or couldn't remember how to
get to a store whose name I had suddenly forgotten, which might have been OK if only I could
have remembered the name of the street where the
store is located.

It isn't bad enough that I have to admit to these
small "lapses," but to add to my frustration, it
seems people who design packages keep thinking
of ways to keep us from opening them. They have
started covering anything and everything you buy

with packaging strong enough to survive an invading enemy attack, making it almost impossible for an unarmed senior to open anything.

Also, "helpful" packagers have started making even dishwashing or laundry more difficult for gentle senior ladies. Unlike my toothpaste, their liquid soap containers come in heavy-to-lift, thick-plastic containers with caps that require you to "squeeze *tightly* and then turn to the right" in order to make the soap ooze out. This is not good news to my Southern, delicate little fingers meant only for lifting a china teacup, with the pinkie finger upright.

Of course, Lord, maybe it's another one of those "blessings in disguise." With all these instructions to follow, maybe I will not accidentally pour laundry soap in the dishwasher or try to brush my teeth with the miracle cream. And, Lord, I realize that if I always followed *your* instructions, maybe it would lead to a healthier, happier life, rejoicing in all your blessings in disguise.

Good, better, bad

Dear Lord, I am happy to report that today I am bad.

Yesterday I had gone from bad to worse and I really felt worse—low and slow, grouchy and grumpy, mad and sad. Today I just feel bad, which is good. I feel good enough to get up and do something that needs doing; and while I'm busy, I will forget to feel worse. So as long as I'm bad already, I might as well do something badder. I'll eat a left-over Halloween candy bar. And then I'll probably eat a second one.

I reported this to a friend on the phone, and she immediately ate a candy bar too. Seniors have to stick together.

Unfortunately, even though we feel strong as a group, it seems that if something unpleasant happens to one of us, it goes viral and something starts happening to others in our group. This month a friend's husband ended up in the hospital. By the time he recovered enough to go home, another friend's wife needed leg surgery. Then allergies kicked in and one of the group could hardly speak, and that was the worst, because we couldn't talk on the phone, discussing the problems of the rest of the group.

Lord, thanks that we still have friends to worry about and share troubles with. Often the best medicine for us is hearing a little joke or a funny story and then sharing it with a friend so we can laugh together. One little story grandparents like is the one about the little boy who rushes up to the teacher's desk, all excited and anxious to tell her, "My grandma is coming to visit us today." The teacher says, "How nice. Where does your grandmother live?" And the little boy says, "Oh, she lives at the airport. Whenever we want her, we just go out and get her."

Or there's the one about the family who had friends in for a fancy dinner, and when they sat down, the sorta frazzled mother asked her little boy to say the blessing. He looked surprised, but his mother urged, "Just say what you've heard Mommy say." And the little boy bowed his head and said, "Dear Lord, why in the world did I invite all these people here for dinner?"

Sorry that I don't have any funnier stories right now, Lord, but maybe that's because today I am bad.

An art show in the neighborhood

Dear Lord, last week when I looked out my window, I saw that my subdivision was featuring a million-dollar art show. Multicolored masterpieces were everywhere I looked. Trees of every species were dressed in bright or muted colors of red, orange, bronze, yellow, and even purple. And as the breeze moved the leaves, they swirled and danced, flirting with the wind. A sight to see.

This week I look out my window, and the yard, the street, and the whole neighborhood are covered with leaves. Yesterday my grandson came in, raggedy-looking and cherry-cheeked from the cold. He said he and some friends from the local college had spent the day raking leaves for senior citizens who couldn't afford to pay someone to do it. What a very good idea, I thought.

Today as I look out, I see my new neighbor across the way dutifully raking and gathering the leaves into a huge mound. Since he and his new bride just moved in last week, I had not met them yet; so I went out to say hello, and he told me he was trying to get a pile of leaves big enough so he could run and jump in like he did as a kid. Just then, his wife came out with a camera, and she and I watched as he grinned and took a leap into the leaves. Then he stood up grinning and held his arms high in a victory, "I did it!" pose. That made my day, thinking we had a new couple in the neighborhood young enough to have that kind of fun.

Autumn leaves teach us so many things—the magnificent beauty of creation, the reminder that there is a time for the beauty to go away until Spring when it will return in a new way, and the idea that there are young people who know how to be of service to others and also how to turn a chore into a leap of fun.

Thank you, Lord, for all the gifts you give us through the year—snow that turns everything into a mystical, white wonderland, golden sunshine that warms the plants to flower and feeds the vegetables to grow into food for us, rain that washes away the muddy places and turns them into glistening mirrors. Of course, beauty does not come free. We pay with snow shoveling, sunburns, and sometimes floods. But it's how we learn that we need to do our part in taking care of the earth you made for us—and how it takes all of us to do that, even senior citizens.

Tuesday mornings

Dear Lord, if it's Tuesday, it must be prayer time at my house. It doesn't seem possible, but for about forty years, a bunch of ladies have come to my house on Tuesday at 9:30 A.M. to start the day with prayer—and therapy.

Today I'm thinking about when it started— when we were young ladies, some with pre-school children in tow. I served coffee and sweet rolls, Kool-Aid, toys, and cookies. Today we are a group of young-at-heart gals with canes and groans and limps but still smiling.

Lord, you remember it began because my wonderful mother had a prayer group that got together every Tuesday morning at her house in Tennessee to pray about whatever was going on back then—war, pestilence, in-laws, children, reci-pes. It lasted for about twenty years, but when my mother died, her group sorta fell apart. You may remember how I felt I should try to carry on her Tuesday tradition but really didn't want to do that. And then I did.

At first, our group was a bit stiff, politely say-ing formal prayers for sick friends, naughty kids, misunderstanding husbands, etc. Perhaps that was because I had only invited ladies I hardly knew—ladies I had met at church or who lived in the neighborhood. And that was because I knew if I asked my really close friends, they would look at me like I had turned into a stranger, and they would just say no.

Blessedly, the group that accepted my invitation kept coming, and we were soon praying about our most secret problems, crying over bad news, rejoicing together over good news, and laughing a lot. We became good friends, and then some of my original close friends began to come too. Through the years, some of the originals have left to go back to work, move away, etc., but when that happens somebody new always shows up to fill the space.

Recently I have heard of several prayer groups similar to ours, and I hope others will have the kind of experiences we have. Tuesday at my house has been the cheapest and the best therapy we could ask for. So thank you, dear Lord, for showing us how prayer can be therapy—and a lot of fun too.

Celebrations

Dear Lord, it's time to get out the balloons and confetti! In today's newspaper there was a headline announcing, "Let's celebrate seniors!" And I thought, "Well, it's about time." But then I read on and realized the celebration the newspaper mentioned would be for star high-school football players who are seniors playing their last hometown school game. Oh well, I DO celebrate those seniors, but even more so, I celebrate some of the seniors I know who are real heroes and heroines.

They have almost insurmountable problems but welcome every new day with grits and honey, as we might say in the South. They might choose cereal for breakfast, like the one known as "grits," and then bravely face whatever pain or difficulty comes their way with the courage known as "true grit." But instead of making everyone aware of their terrible senior challenges, they choose to treat each insurmountable with the touch of honey known as prayer and a smile.

Of course, senior problems can go from minor inconveniences to truly terrible suffering; and everyone's pain threshold is different, so we can't judge others. For example, some might think going through a round of rehabbing exercises is torture, and some might think trying to eat a bowl of grits is torture.

So, Lord, remind us seniors to be more thoughtful of other seniors. Give us a nudge to look around and find a way to celebrate the seniors we know who have that great "grin and bear it" reaction to whatever "senior surprises" they encounter. It doesn't have to be a big thing—maybe sending them a cheery or funny card or calling for a telephone chat or buying a cake or pie and taking it (or get someone not-so-old to take it) to their door as a surprise as we tell them "It's Celebrating Seniors Day!"

And, Lord, I know it may not be nice to celebrate yourself, but I'm a senior, and today I think I really should treat me with the rest of that ice cream that is in my freezer just waiting for a celebration!

Tooth fairy fun

Dear Lord, this morning I had to leave home and report in at the House of Horrors. I had to go to the dentist. I mentioned this to a friend, and she said, "It just isn't fair. When little kids lose a tooth, they just put the old tooth under a pillow and the tooth fairy shows up to give them money. And then a new tooth magically appears in the place of the old one and serves dutifully for many years to come. What is wrong with this picture? Seniors lose teeth, so where are *our* tooth fairies?"

Lord, I have been meditating on what my friend said. When we oldsters have a tooth go bad, we can't just tie a piece of string to it and then tie the other end of the string to a door knob and slam the door to pull the tooth. No, it takes pain and money to get the old tooth out and then even more money to get a new tooth "built" in its stead. It just isn't fair!

Well, as usual, I shouldn't complain. I have a wonder-working dentist whose aim in life seems to be to save every little bit of every tooth I have left. He sees my "canine" teeth crumbling, and he commands them, "Sit! Stay!" And when an unholy hole or crack appears, he stirs up a magic potion to fill it up or smooth it over. And thus my teeth allow me to chew and talk and smile—if I do it very carefully. So I was grateful for that—but then my tooth fairy *did* show up!

Every ten years or so, as you know, Lord, my church invites parishioners to have their photos taken; and then the photos are printed, along with names, addresses and phone numbers, in a parish directory. This directory is very helpful when you are trying to put together a meeting or event and need to find members to help. So we all look forward to receiving the new directory.

This year, when I had my photo taken, I had a huge smile on my face, since my grandson had agreed to be pictured with me. And when the photographer asked if we would like to have the photo "embellished" in any way, I laughingly said, "Oh, I sure would like it if you could make my terrible old teeth look better." I forgot about it until the directory arrived, and there I was, with pearly whites perfect enough to star in a toothpaste ad! It was a miracle! The photographer had taken me at my word and become my very own tooth fairy.

So thank you, Lord, for dentists and directories and tooth fairies and miracles around every corner.

Senior trivia

Dear Lord, recently, due to my "scientific research," I have discovered some fascinating facts that have something in common with seniors, and I will no doubt repeat these (maybe once too much) to my friends. For example, I did not know that giraffes, like many seniors, have high blood pressure. In the case of the giraffes, it takes pressure to get that blood to travel up their looong necks—just like some seniors may need pressure from friends or family to follow their doctor's advice, take their medicine, and eat wisely.

Next, I often watch birds soaring high into the sky but did not know that birds can't survive in outer space! That's because their digestive system is dependent on gravity, which does not work in space. Most seniors could not survive in outer space, because NASA would probably not okay accepting a senior to take the course to become an astronaut.

Everyone knows that an octopus has eight arms, but I did not know they have three hearts! Many seniors seem to have three hearts because they have children, grandchildren, grandchildren's friends, and maybe even great-grandchildren whom they worry about and try to help with a listening, caring ear, bits of money, if-asked-for advice, and lots of prayer. Some of them could also use eight arms to give enough hugs to go around.

But there's more. In Russia, some stray but smart dogs ride subways, somehow knowing where to get off—in areas with the most plentiful food supplies. Some even "commute," riding in for the day and coming back to their "home" area in the evening. Seniors in this town (like me) can't ride the subways, since our city has none, but we do sometimes travel away to other subdivisions where there are more plentiful supplies of garage sales. And we do come home in the evening.

Well, Lord, enough fun facts for today; so thanks again for giraffes and birds and the eight-armed oc- topus and even stray dogs—and their strange con- nections with seniors. Your world is filled with so many amazing things and real "scientific research- ers" who seek out the facts and give me the fun of hearing about them. Bless them all.

Stuck in nothingness

Dear Lord, today I feel "bone tired." I had a good night's sleep, but I wanted to keep sleeping. I felt too tired and weak to walk to the mailbox in the front yard and send off the cards and bills I addressed yesterday. I made myself "post" the mail, but I came back in and barely made it to my favorite rocking chair. Here I sit like a blob. I would really like a cup of tea, but it would be too hard to follow the well-used recipe—"place teabag in cup, boil water in the microwave, add water to teabag, stir." No, no, that would just be too hard to do. So I continue stuck in my nothingness.

Lord, most days I start slowly, but soon I can switch from "slow gear" to "drive gear" to "go" gear, and I make it through the day. Not today. I just want to sit and read a book or work a crossword puzzle and then get up enough energy to walk to the bedroom to take a nap.

Oh well, no one is waiting for me to put out a forest fire or cook a Thanksgiving dinner or save a puppy from dashing into traffic. My friends tell me they have days like this too. Maybe after I indulge in that nap and a snack or a big chocolate bar, I will put on my Wonder Woman cape and do something daring, like going out on the patio to sit and meditate.

Meditating will either make me sleepy again or fill me with enough gumption to get up and do some small but necessary household chore. I might even start thinking up some new ideas about simpler ways to do things I could do or should do. Maybe I will get so busy thinking that I will forget the knee bone and the hip bone and the neck bone and the head bone and think more about the funny bone. Recalling a good joke or something funny that happened recently might give me a chuckle and remind me that I still have more good days than bony ones. So thank you, Lord, that I also have more free time than most, time to get on those old knee bones in prayer. I love you, Lord.

Traveling, senior class

Dear Lord, this morning, all I can say is Ahhh, the amazing Amalfi Coast. I am surrounded with warm, golden sunshine as I travel to Apulia, Alberobello, and Baroque Lecce, discover the enchanting village of Polignano a Mare, weave though charming byways and piazzas, and stop to say a prayer in a basilica by the sea.

Of course, I am not traveling by jet today but by rocking chair. This happens every time I get one of those colorful travel brochures in the mail, inviting me to take an "educational journey of a lifetime." Like a lot of seniors, even if my MasterCard could handle such costly travel, my spirit is willing but my knees are not. But that's OK. I enjoy reading about places that I am not ever going to visit.

Luckily, I have already visited some amazing places—the Statue of Liberty, the Parthenon (not the one in Greece but the one in Nashville, Tennessee), the St. Louis Arch, the Grand Canyon, and of course, Disneyland!

Lord, I am so grateful that even if I don't fly far away these days, my imagination is still working OK and my knotty knees still get me to the grocery, to luncheons with the ladies, to an occasional concert, and even to a fancy French restaurant that happens to be a few blocks from my home where I can find the kind of exotic pastries and desserts I may have enjoyed on one of those luxury cruises.

Ah, yes, Lord, I am so blessed. I can still imagine discovering lovely places with unpronounceable names and where I can still pretend that those desserts are calorie-free. And I can still enjoy the golden sunshine that finds its way all the way from the Amalfi Coast to my backyard.

Mixed-up meandering

Dear Lord, I used to tell people that I had a mixed marriage. That was because my husband was a Civil War fan and loved to read about it, talk about it, and buy lots of books about it. So he was sometimes living in the past. My son was only interested in computers and outer space, so he was living in the future. And here I was, stuck in the middle, trying to take care of everything in the present. I thought of that today when an interesting article in the newspaper came to my attention. It explained that no human being—from cave dweller to astronaut—has ever lived in the past. We have each lived only in our own present.

So much for the saying that many old folks "live in the past!" We may remember the past fondly (or not), but we are too busy trying to find how to make the most of our present. It isn't easy when your arm doesn't want to fit into a sleeve and your leg has forgotten how to bend enough to slip into a stocking and your head bone's batteries are running low and your big toe is sending "ouch" signals about those new shoes you liked so much.

Yes, I know; as usual, I am exaggerating—and

exasperating—today, Lord. You've heard it all before. Now that I have used up some of my precious present, I see the sun is beckoning me to get outside and stop singing the blues so I can figure out which direction to go today—visit a friend who is ailing, buy a small bouquet of mixed-color flowers for my kitchen table, look for a looser pair of shoes, or maybe just find a restaurant that still makes banana splits with three mixed flavors of ice cream.

Thanks again, Lord, for the way you wrap all my "presents" with your love.

Angels on guard

Dear Lord, when I was thumbing through a magazine today, I noticed a mention of "Gardening Angels"—a group of neighbors who get together each summer to grow a vegetable garden and share the "fruits of their labor"—not only among their group but also with others they know who need help paying for groceries. It is such a good idea, especially for seniors who sometimes have more spare time than they can fill.

I once grew delicious tomatoes in a small plot off the patio, but I'm afraid my digging days are over. However, the mention of angels reminded me of one of the many times my husband "blindsided" me. We were playing bridge with new friends we didn't know very well, and when the subject of angels came up, my husband said, "Oh, I saw my guardian angel one time."

What? He *saw* an angel? He very seriously explained that he was on a train, sleeping in a small bed they then called a "berth." He woke up in the middle of the night, and "his" angel was sitting on the edge of the berth; and he was wearing a tuxedo!

What? While I was having a panic attack, sure my husband and I would never see these new friends again, the other lady spoke up and said, "Oh, I'm so glad you said that because I never told anybody about it but I saw *my* guardian angel once too—and she was very beautiful." Her husband looked at me, and we didn't know whether to laugh or cry or start to wonder how long it takes to get a divorce. So we just went on with the bridge game.

On the way home I asked my husband why he never told me about his angel before, and he said, "I don't know. I just never thought to mention it until tonight."

Well, Lord, though I have never seen my guardian angel, I know he or she is very busy, saving me from so many near misses and oops moments almost every day. So thank you, Lord, for the gift of angels and for a husband who kept my life interesting, because he was always full of surprises.

Senior growth

Dear Lord, I was thinking today about how most kids always want to be older and taller. They say, "I'm two and a half…I'm three going on four…on my birthday I will be five." And in the past, parents would find a door jamb or a place on the wall where the kid would come and stretch to stand as tall as possible, and the parent would put a ruler across the top of the kid's head and draw a pencil to mark their height. Every month or so, they would continue the "ritual," and the kids would get measured again to see how much they had grown. Maybe they still do that. I hope they do.

Adults don't draw lines on a wall, but they often "mark" how much their bank account has grown or how much they have accomplished in their chosen work or if they have achieved the next step up the ladder of so-called success.

Now, seniors aren't anxious to get older (even though we sometimes brag about it), and we would probably like to be taller, since we all seem to be shrinking. But with all this "marking," I am thinking, how often do we measure or mark how much we have grown in faith?

Are we more or less excited about the presence of God in our life? Have the "rituals" become so familiar that we take them for granted? Have we grown beyond yesteryear in our prayer life or our understanding of God? Or, maybe, have we lost the excitement we once felt about our religion and the "miracles" you, God, have strewn in our lives?

Well, why am I sitting here questioning others about what kind of faith marks they have made or might consider making when I am guilty, Lord, guilty? There are lots of marks on the walls of my house, but they are marking the negligence of the resident house cleaner and not her growth in faith.

Before I test anybody else, I'd better think deeply myself. I know I'm older and shorter, but "how have I grown in faith?" Maybe only you, Lord, know the real answer to that.

Sharing likes and dislikes

Dear Lord, today with the help of my usual cup of steaming, soothing coffee, I finally managed to unhinge my creaky bones enough to get out my trusty calendar to see where and when I am supposed to be today. Not surprisingly, my calendar is filled with old-folks happenings—visits to the doctor or dentist, time to push the cart at the grocery, time to push the panic button to make myself do something positive instead of looking in the mirror and scaring myself with that face that ain't what it used to be. But today's event is a good one. It's Book Discussion day.

Many moons ago I saw a little sign in our neighborhood bookstore, asking if anyone would like to start a book group. About twenty people did, and our mismatched group still gets together once a month—to share ideas, viewpoints, likes, and dislikes of a variety of books.

Now I've noticed that a number of seniors are joining or starting book clubs. They start some in neighborhoods or churches or just among a bunch of friends. They choose a date to meet, usually once a month, then they all read the same book and then gather to talk about it. Having a deadline makes you read old books you always meant to read or new ones that just came out. And making the old brain work faster can help you learn something new and have fun at the same time.

Thank you, Lord, for sending me to "my" group, who are now "close acquaintances" more than close friends, but we are always glad to see and learn from each other. It makes me get out of the house and stir some brain waves so I can share and compare thoughts and experiences with others. It opens a window to let in fresh ideas instead of just ideas about how to get that fly that keeps circling my piece of coffee cake.

Oh, that reminds me, Lord. I've been meaning to ask you. Why did you find it necessary to create and then send us those flies? Actually, I've been meaning to ask you a lot of things, but that will have to wait for another time. I have to go now or I'll be late for our book discussion meeting.

Step lightly

Dear Lord, this morning, the daily paper made me feel so young! There was an article about something that even I, as old as I am, never heard of before—public bath houses. At a time when only a few people were starting to have a bit of indoor plumbing, most everyone counted on the big washtub in the middle of the kitchen for an occasional bath. So it seems some cities opened public bath spots where you could spend three cents and get a bar of soap and a towel and take a shower. And if you were very modest, they would even provide a swim suit for you so your bath would not be quite so public.

To my surprise, my city still has a very nice Art Deco building that was once the municipal bath house but is now owned and used for storage by a man who once biked there as a kid for an occasional three-cent treat.

Lord, today some large houses have as many bathrooms as bedrooms, and they are as luxurious as old-time "living rooms." Most regular houses today have bathrooms that can be large, small, or luxurious but are *all* a real challenge for any senior who happens to want to take a relaxing soak, a quick shower, or a bubble bath. Thankfully, clever workers can install "grab bars" or different kinds of bathroom "furniture" to make senior life a bit less challenging.

Lord, I'm sorry that I've been taking up your time today chatting about bath houses and bathrooms. I shouldn't bother you with my many little newspaper discoveries, but this one leads me to pray that today's society will start to pay more attention to clean living and clean insides instead of just clean outsides.

Dear Lord, I am very grateful that I live in a time when I can carefully have a bath or shower (without a swim suit) whenever I want—even though one of those looong, lazy showers probably does cost more than three cents to pay for the hot water. But always remind us seniors, Lord, to remember that no matter how fancy or luxurious a bathroom may be, it is always slippery and dangerous, so we should always remember the old saying, "Watch Your Step!"

Young vs. senior surprises

Dear Lord, there are no college classes today, so I can spend a bit more time with my six-foot-three grandson, who always lights up my days when he comes running into the house saying "Hey Banna, give me a hug."

When he first moved into my house, I hoped to teach him how to start to be an adult, but he has taught me so many things I never dreamed of. He has given me a peek into his world of youth and newness and, yes, religion and possibilities and a different way of viewing the world and its variety of people. Hopefully, we are widening horizons for each other in a good way.

Dear Lord, please help me open my mouth when I need to uphold my beliefs and standards, *and* help me keep it closed when I start to criticize or challenge his side of the story. Teach me to wait until I think it through and choose a better moment to bring it up for discussion later.

Lord, when the opportunity came for me to share my home with my college-age grandson, I was afraid. We had always had fun together but it was on short visits when I went to California or he came to visit my St. Louis home. 24-7 together is something else.

We eased into it. I did not have a heart attack when he drove my car, and he didn't choke when I served a recipe he never ate before. We juggled his school schedule and my senior goings and comings—and so far it has been a challenge and a real blessing for both of us.

It's hard for seniors to adjust to all of the new ways, the new music, and the new ideas about everything. I tell my friends that living with a handsome, friendly, fun-loving grandson will either make me feel young again or age me very fast. With his busy schedule of school, work, and friends, I never know when he is going to charge into the house, full of stories about where he has been or how his day has gone or something surprising he has discovered in this new town where he has landed.

Thank you, Lord, for such sweet surprises.

Goodnight, God

Dear Lord, I saw a sign today that really got my attention. It read, "What if you woke up today with only the things you thanked God for yesterday?" Oh boy, I would be in a lot of trouble. I didn't thank you, Lord, for my toothbrush, the microwave oven, a warm sweater, a cold drink, any kind of clothing or shoes or chocolate or keys to the car. Well, maybe I thanked you for chocolate. Even my senior forgetfulness wouldn't have stopped me from thanking you for chocolate.

What *did* I speak to you about yesterday? I probably mentioned my son and my grandson. As an all-knowing mother, I always think they need help. And they probably think I too need lots of help. I often thank you for my nice warm bed and a fluffy pillow to help me snooze happily through the night. I probably said grace for what I had to eat, but I don't really remember what that was. And I did not thank you for my house or my car or my Social Security number or my insurance policy. Oh no! I'm sure I did not say thank you for my credit cards. How could I live without them?!

Yes, I would be in big trouble. And I bet a lot of

other people would be too. Actually, seniors might be in better shape than younger ones. Many young people seem to think the world owes them anything they want—and they have the bills to prove it. The older you get, even if you have less, the more you have to be thankful for—family, friends, enough food to sustain you, a place to live. And yes, one more day to wake up alive!

Maybe I will ask my friends today what they thanked God for last night. I wonder if they will remember. Maybe their prayers will be an inspiration for me. Whatever, Lord, this got me thinking, and I guess I should be really careful what I thank you for tonight, just in case.

But Lord, all these years, you have provided for me. You have gifted me with so many blessings. You have given me so many joys and surprises that I would have never thought to ask for myself. Lord, maybe you are everybody's best personal shopper. You know what we need, and you give it to us or help us get it for ourselves. Sometimes we are too stupid to be grateful, but you keep on giving.

So, Lord, thank you. What can I give you in return? All I have to offer are my prayers and my love.

Family picnics

Dear Lord, this is an off day—no errands to run, no laundry to wash, no flowers to plant, no grocery visits needed—and I am so glad. I just want to sit in my rocker and think about yesterday and the tradition of family picnics. Some have huge get-togethers that take a lot of planning and are a lot of fun. Our tradition was very small, since we had no relatives within earshot of our home, but it was still a lot of fun.

At a time when I was a harried housewife and my husband had a demanding job, in the good old summertime we would seek deliverance by occasionally heading for the park. I would pack the car with my Southern-fried chicken and various things in little containers—potato salad, stuffed eggs, or whatever. Then I would add some reading material, two fold-up easy chairs, and cold lemonade. My husband would come home from work, hang up his business suit and business problems, throw on something comfortable, and jump in the car. By then, I would have also packed up our five-year-old son and his best friend and some of their toys. We would drive around the park until we found a shady quiet place with a picnic table and unload.

After we had feasted, the kids would erupt as though they had been held in captivity for many days, and off they would go to explore the nearby and make up their own private games. My husband and I would lounge in the folding chairs, reading and chatting and enjoying the cool, cool lemonade.

But that was long ago. Now my son and his son are all grown up, but every summer, like yesteryears, I will get a telephone call from my son— "Mom, the weather's nice today. Let's have a picnic." Of course, it's a bit different now. I no longer slave over a hot stove to make the Southern-fried chicken since we can buy that with all the "fixings" to go. All I have to take along is a plastic tablecloth! We still enjoy the food and the fun and the great outdoors. Some traditions—even the small ones—linger on.

I was just thinking, Lord, that once you kinda had a really big family picnic when everybody ate loaves and fishes instead of fried chicken. As always, you left us an important lesson that day. So thank you again, Lord, for lessons and families and picnics and plastic tablecloths.

Magic moments

Dear Lord, this morning, I have been sitting on my patio, basking in the sun, enjoying the occasional breeze that flits by—and feeling sorry for some of today's youth. I am relaxing and rejoicing because I am reading a new book and I love it. But I hate that so many young people today spend most of their time with machines, so they don't know what they are missing. They seem to think reading is a chore, something that you have to do for school so you can get a mark good enough to graduate and be released from the "punishment" of learning.

A lot of us older folk know how sad that is because we have learned the magic of a book. It can take you to explore the Amazon or the Great Barrier Reef, let you ride a camel on the Sahara Desert, or go to Paris for dinner atop the Eiffel Tower. It can invite you to any kind of fairy-tale experience you might dream about. Reading can help you forget that your knee hurts or your shoulder needs therapy. And "touring" the library for a book of your choice can be a free vacation.

Many oldsters (like me) can find magic moments inside the covers of old or new books. And if you're lucky, you might find some valuable information you can pass on to others to spike up the usual senior conversation. For example, this morning I read a bit of trivia that gave me a giggle for the day. Did you know that once upon a time, it was against the law in Nicholas County, West Virginia, for clergymen to tell funny stories from the pulpit? I don't know about others, but sometimes I would enjoy a bit of haha in the homily. So, Lord, thank you today for the invention of the printing press and for wise and/or funny people who know how to put words on paper that teach or entertain. And, Lord, forgive me if I didn't spend enough time today reading *your* "good" book. I'll try to do better tomorrow.

Space ships and casseroles

Dear Lord, this morning I came across a list someone made of "the five best toys of all time"—a box,
a stick, string, a cardboard tube, and dirt. Way in the
mists of my past, I remember that my kindergarten
son used all those items in the "space ship" he was
building in our basement. He and his best friend
(the boy next door who was the same age) spent
many happy hours in it "blasting off" to discover
new planets and wage war on other space ships.
Whenever my husband and I had adult friends visit-
ing, my son would quietly take the hand of one of
them and say, "Would you like to see my space ship
in the basement?" Who could resist?

That pile of boxes and lots of string was probably not as exciting to our friends as it was to my
son, but he loved it because God had given him
the best toy of all—the gift of imagination.

Today's kids are exposed to so many exciting,
expensive toys that I pray they will still have room
for the "five best" ones. And it's the same with
grown-ups and seniors. We are all so immersed in
the television world of "too much is not enough."

Dear Lord, help us all turn off the media's idea

of happiness and rejoice in big or small blessings. Let us think of senior days as casseroles. Once we always made our own special casserole with the same ingredients, and it was delicious; but when the grocery budget ran low, we might not have *all* we needed, so we used what we had, and it was different—maybe not as good but sometimes surprisingly delicious. Let's not focus on what was but on what is and use that wonderful gift of imagination to make it surprisingly good enough.

Thermometer alert

Dear Lord, my husband once told me my personal thermometer was broken. Like most people, he felt hot, cold, warm, or cool, depending on the season. But not me. Summer, spring, winter, and fall, I feel chilly if I don't have layering. And it isn't because I'm old. It's been this way for years. In my house and car and most everywhere I travel—grocery, movie, restaurant, friend's house, church—the air conditioning does not match my condition.

Now today's nip in the air tells me it's time for more layering. Even in summer I end up adding a light sweater or summer jacket wherever I go. But October signals that the time is coming when I will have to start thinking about heavy sweaters, coat, hat, gloves, snow boots, etc. So many woolies give me the willies, but if I forget the layers, I end up with sniffles and snorts, sneezing and wheezing.

Well, I don't know why I am welcoming this lovely season of the year by complaining. I should be rejoicing in all the layers of colors you use to paint my world. And I do rejoice. I love the brilliant reds and pinks and oranges of fall flowers, leaves and trees, and so many golden sunsets.

Thanks, Lord, for layer cakes, egg-layer hens, layettes for babies, and the laymen and women who do so much good work in our churches. And forgive me for being a lay-about today. I'm gonna get up and get out right now and soak up the beauty. But first, I'd better grab a little sweater to take along.

Ring-a-ling

Dear Lord, I've just discovered a new exercise routine that I've been doing for years without realizing it. I know I'm old enough to remember that my grandma had a party-line telephone, so that can be a clue that I am not young enough to have a smart phone or an omnipresent, omniscient, never-leave-your-side phone.

I have the kind of phone that keeps ringing until you run from the kitchen or the patio or the basement to grab the phone that you left on the sofa or across the room, smirking next to the rocking chair. All that just to hear a stranger say, "Congratulations. You have just won a trip to Zanzibar."

Actually, my old talk-box may be saving my life because I have to keep in shape in order to run fast enough and far enough to make that ringing stop! It is probably entertaining for anyone to watch the didoes I do, running to answer this unsmart phone, but I still cannot convince myself to get a phone that can text and twitter and sneer at me because we don't speak the same language.

I am usually ready to try something new (even

though I really don't want to go to Zanzibar), and I know many of my "old" friends have gone to the dark side and now flaunt their newest phone wherever we go. But they'll be sorry, missing out on my healthy exercise routine. No, no, they won't. They are the friends who also go to the gym or some kind of exercise club. And I don't do that either. Maybe I'd better get my act together.

Probably it's only old folk like me who hate the idea of having a constant companion phone. But why do I need one? With my old phone, I can have long conversations with friends and relatives near or far, make doctors' appointments, and purchase strange things from the catalogs I receive in the Pony Express snail mail. But I guess I could do all that with a new phone too, and maybe I could even learn to speak new phone language, and maybe in turn, it could save me from breaking a leg with all those exciting didoes.

Thanks again, Lord, for the old and the new and for trying to teach me which one to choose. But I hope it's OK if you and I continue to just talk and not twitter.

Music lesson

Dear Lord, a long time ago, in a memory far, far away, the one thing I wanted most to do was learn how to play the piano. We didn't have a piano. And piano lessons for me were probably not on the top of my folks' cash outflow list. But none of that seemed important. I could see myself in a fancy evening gown taking bows for my masterful performance before a cheering audience. Of course, I guess I was maybe five or six years old at the time. Gradually I found other interests, but the memory must have stayed hidden in the attic of my head.

I worked my way into a small "career" in advertising, got married, and had a son who graduated from Notre Dame and then sailed away from home as a Navy lieutenant. Then he got married, and I became a grandmother, and my husband retired and read books, and I wrote books. That's when I came across an article that suggested seniors should always find something NEW to do or volunteer for or explore. That would be the way to keep young—by challenging yourself to learn something different. I agreed with that, and the door creaked open when I saw an ad with a picture of a lovely piano and the headline, "Adult Piano Lessons." Maybe I could still take that bow someday.

I tried. I really did. I even learned how to play one song—"When the Saints Come Marching In"—not exactly the symphonic music that requires a fancy evening gown. But I did achieve the goal of learning something new. I learned that my fingers can fly over the keys of my computer much better than they can "tickle the old ivories" on a piano.

Many seniors have followed the good advice to get out and find something new to make life more interesting. If they are still driving, they can volunteer to give non-driving seniors a ride to church or wherever, visit shut-ins, volunteer at a hospital to push old people in wheelchairs or even be a driver to deliver Meals on Wheels. Some who are no longer "mobile" can find a prayer partner to share prayers every day on the telephone or to make it a habit to call other shut-ins just to chat once a week.

Lord, I am thinking...wouldn't it be wonderful if all seniors could start something new just by looking around for ways to share whatever time we have wherever help is needed? In that way, we could all make beautiful music together.

Weak willies

Dear Lord, in my "past life," I have often felt "weak in the knees," usually when I had to be the "speaker" at a luncheon or a meeting. I was always afraid I would forget what I planned to say or mix up the "cue cards" I carried to remind me. Since I was always expected to say something humorous, I was afraid nobody would laugh when I said something that was supposed to be funny. But I had lots of kind and generous audiences, and they were the type who liked to laugh, so all went well. Afterward, I would chide myself for feeling weak in the knees, but the next time I would do it again.

There were also other times when I had good reason to be weak in the knees—when I had to go to the hospital for some kind of small operation or when I had to drive alone to a distant city in very bad weather or when I decided to go and get my hair cut really short! I knew that feeling weak was foolish because everything always, with your help, Lord, turned out OK—except those haircuts.

Of course, "feeling weak in the knees" is not the only way to suggest fear. Being scared could be described as having my heart go pitty-pat—which does happen when I look through my purse and think I have lost my credit card. Before I fall into a faint, I look through the purse more carefully, and there it is—not lost, even though it should be so I couldn't use it so happily. Or I could say something was so scary, it made my hair turn white overnight—which does not happen only because of Lady Clairol. But now that seniority has settled in, feeling weak in the knees is no longer just a figure of speech. It's a daily reality.

So, Lord, thank you for different ways to use words and thank you for pain pills and rocking chairs and cups of hot tea and friends who don't mind sharing stories of the miseries.

And, Lord, even though it pains me to do so, I should even thank you for the weak knees since they do still get me to lots of places I want to go.

Musing munching

Dear Lord, yesterday some of the "girls" had lunch together, and we began talking about how today's TV shows are so different than the old ones, and we all remembered the show about how kids say the darndest things. One little girl who had had an "owie" said, "I don't know why God made people so breakable. I had to have three stitches and a shot to get put back together." We seniors can agree.

Someone's grandson had said, "Today they taught us that Edison made light. But at church they told us that God made light. Did Edison steal the idea from God?"

Another kid said, "I have been trying to read the Bible but I can't find out what the word 'begat' means. No one will tell me."

On Halloween, a little girl told her grandma, "My Mom got me a devil costume to wear to trick-or-treat. Do you think that will make God mad?"

One animal lover asked, "Did God really make an elephant like that or was it an accident?" And another asked, "Do animals talk to God like we do, or is there somebody else for them?"

Well, we had a lot of laughs with our lunch

today. And we went home thinking about how children have such innocent and interesting ideas about God. But some seniors have unusual ideas too—like about how God let the process of aging get out of hand.

OK, God, I admit it. I often ask you or discuss with you even stranger ideas than those of the kids. But today was great, and it probably started us girls thinking of a lot more stories of "God, as seen by kids."

My favorite memory of today was the one when a grandmother remembered the time her little granddaughter said, "Grandma, I don't ever feel so all alone any more, now that I learned more about God."

Some seniors might not agree with that when they are having a really bad, mad, sickly, alone day. Like me, they might even say some of the darndest things to you, Lord! But we'll get over it. We seniors have had enough good days and good laughs to remind us we are never really all alone.

Stumped or surprised

Dear Lord, today I was stumped. Stumped by a riddle I never heard before. "What is greater than God—and more evil than the devil? The poor have it. The rich need it. And if you eat it, you will die."

Well, some of today's fashionable ladies are so thin you might think they look at anything with a calorie and think "if you eat it, you will die"—but they do look stylish in their size #1 or #2 outfits. The poor have nothing but are often happier than the rich who need nothing until they make a bad stock purchase. And the devil is the most evil, but some of today's TV programs are running a close second.

As we grow older and wiser (?), Lord, sometimes all modern life seems like a riddle. Everything is so complicated. You can't deal with the Internet until you remember which password goes with whatever it is you are trying to find. If you go grocery shopping you have to listen to the shopper in aisle two who is telling someone on her "smart" phone details of her recent hospital visit, and the man in aisle three who is speaking on his not-so-smart-phone as he reads aloud all the labels on all of the cans, trying to find which one his wife wants him to bring home. And in the meantime, you are heading for aisle four, hoping to magically spot all the items you wrote on the little yellow pad you left lying on the kitchen table. It's a jungle out there, Lord.

Forgive us old codgers for criticizing others who are more socially tuned in to the technical rhythms of today's world. Help us keep in mind that we will never be stumped if we remember that *nothing* is the answer to that riddle.

And thank you, Lord, that we don't need a password to reach you wherever we are, even when we are grocery shopping.

Silver threads

Dear Lord, I was looking around the house today, trying to see what I should dust or what I should thrust out the door so I won't have to dust it. My eyes lit up when I noticed the lovely silver pieces we were given at our wedding long, long ago. Unlike some friends, I have actually enjoyed polishing the silver. I could clean the whole house and nobody would notice, but if I polished the silver, you could really tell the difference. And I really did use our silver because we liked to have lots of little parties or get-togethers, and I enjoyed having flowers and a properly "set" table with all the silver trimmings. That was "back in the day," when I also actually enjoyed finding fancy recipes to fill the fancy dishes.

Today I realized it has been a while since I used a silver tray. Now it seems too fancy to even use a real china plate instead of a paper plate to serve carry-out food or frozen microwave dinners. But I still have "the ladies" in at least a couple times a year for a festive get-together, so that will give me one more chance to polish the silver.

Thinking about how those little "extras" made me feel luxurious through the years, I began to remember the many kinds of parties we enjoyed—birthday parties, of course, and Thanksgiving dinners and Christmas get-togethers, but there were so many others. We had a traveling party where appetizers and Hawaiian drinks were served in the living room, then the main meal—Beef Stroganoff—downstairs in the "rathskellar," then ooh-la-la French desert with coffee in the dining room (all served with "the good silver").

We always had a Halloween party for adults every year, where the "gang" came up with the funniest and most original costumes; and we still have a lot of laughs remembering how the guys dressed as everything from a housewife to Sherlock Holmes. And New Year's Day meant football viewing with snacks and then big bowls of bean soup with home-made corn bread (not served with silver).

Dear Lord, it's funny how the idea of something "special" changes. Many of today's young housewives would consider a silver piece to be junk instead of joy, the way I consider some of their music to be dreadful noise instead of joyful ear candy. Help us, Lord, to try to understand change and accept the good and make peace with the not-so-good, being careful to know the difference.

Say it isn't snow

Dear Lord, this morning I rushed to the window and Oh! What to my wondering eyes did appear? No, not reindeer. Snowflakes! No matter how late each year on the calendar snow appears out my window, I am always surprised. It could be Christmas Eve and I would still say, "Snow already?"

I am not a fan of snow. Oh, I love to watch the fluffy flakes drift softly down, turning my yard into a winter wonderland. But that icy cold stuff also coats my driveway and surrounding streets and highways, turning my world into a "Danger! No Trespassing" sign.

Sleigh bells ring, are you listening—to the caution alerts to watch where you step? No dancing on the black ice or the slick brick walk on the way to your mailbox, no sloshing out to the bird feeder surrounded by snow and trimmed with icicle fringe. Take care, beware.

It's a shame that something so beautiful can be so dangerous for senior citizens. We all may have fun memories of snowmen, snowball fights, and even snow ice cream—which is now forbidden because of air pollution. But that was then, and this is now, and for the moment I am focusing on the sight out my window where the beautiful white snow has covered all the scruffy places in my backyard and turned them into fabulous ice sculptures.

Lord, in the midst of all this beauty, I remember that those scruffy places are just hiding; and when the sun's warmth takes away their hiding place, they will still need for me to clean them up. And, oh-oh, my senior consciousness starts waking up to remind me how often today's culture tries to cover our world's scruffiness by hiding it behind the glitzy, shiny, "beautiful" temptations of today. It's gonna take a really big snow plow and a lot of work and prayer to clean up that snow job.

Well, Lord, enough criticism. I am going to try to act my age today, obey the snow no-nos, and not do anything flaky. I will sit by my window, enjoying the beautiful snowy views outside while I am snug and safe inside with my cup of tea. Help us, Lord, with the cleanups; and thank you for snowflakes and memories and the wonderful people in the world who work every day in every way to turn our scruffy planet back to the wonderland you created it to be.

Second childhood

Dear Lord, I love watching a child bent over a coloring book, deep in concentration, working to turn out a masterpiece good enough to go on the refrigerator door. And recently I've been introduced to a new idea being welcomed by many "wanna-be artists," of various ages, especially seniors. The new hot-sellers are coloring books for adults.

Now these are not the cartoon kind of pictures that children like to fill in with bright colors while trying to "stay in the lines." The adult books go from very easy designs to more difficult ones, all just waiting for the "artist" to bring them to life with interesting mixes of different bold or pastel colors. You might use colored pencils or the traditional crayons and you can choose simple designs at first before you "graduate" to the more fanciful ones. Some are beautiful intricate or geometric designs that can be fun to do and good enough to send as home-made greeting cards.

One lady said she was proud to call herself a lifelong doodler, and now she has found that adult coloring can be a different way to relax, reduce stress, increase concentration, and decrease anxiety.

Lord, we seniors sometimes need all those things; but first, we will need to let go of what we think of as "acceptable adult behavior" and allow ourselves to have some fun playing with crayons like the kids.

Lord, I was never very good at "staying in the lines" as a kid or a grownup, so I still am sometimes accused of doing something deemed by others as *not* "acceptable adult behavior." Therefore, no one will be surprised if I get myself to a bookstore and buy myself a new coloring book. They *will* be surprised if I manage to turn out some acceptable senior art.

Maybe I will get books for my friends and challenge them to try something old/new for fun. In the past, seniors might have felt slightly insulted when someone told them "You're in your second childhood." Today that might be a compliment for anyone who has discovered coloring books for adults. Thank you, Lord, for all of life's new discoveries!

Sunday songs

Dear Lord, the music in church this morning was beautiful as usual. Today in one hymn I really noticed the words "All we have and all that we offer...comes from a heart both frightened and free." The words seemed appropriate for seniors.

I don't think "all that we have" means just money. Seniors have so much more to offer.

We have memories to share with our grandchildren or someone else's grandchildren who are interested in history and wonder what it was like way back when. Once you get their attention, some are in awe about how really different life was just a generation back. Different food or songs or jokes or stories about some unusual family happenings might catch their ears.

Retirees might be able to volunteer to share some business experiences. Housewives have stories about how they grew up and how their mother cooked on a stove that used wood.

But the lines that really caught my ears were "Comes from a heart both frightened and free." When you get "old" (which is a different age for everyone since it has to do with how you see yourself), you may be frightened by the future since you have never been that "old" before. You had a certain lifestyle and you were used to it, but now it gets changed. You may need a cane or a crutch or a wheelchair or be as fleet of foot as ever. You may have to move from your home to a different one or stop driving the car or get hearing aids or new eyeglasses. And any or all of this is frightening.

But you are also free. You don't have all the responsibilities as before. You don't have to do or go or act or worry about a lot of things that took up your life. You are free to live the same life as always, with a few difficulties, or you can do things you never got to do or wished to do or hoped to do, or you can stop doing things you never wanted to do.

Well, probably a lot of seniors would not agree with me about the necessary lifestyle changes that come with each year. Everyone has different ideas about change. Each new day may be a chore or an opportunity.

O, Lord, help us who have earned our seniority. Show us the way you want us to use each new day you give us. Teach us how to use "all that we have and all that we offer," and be with us in this frightening but free time of life.

A fishy tale

Dear Lord, until this morning, I never thought about, read about, or wanted to know about any kind of fish except the can of tuna in my pantry. But now a headline informs me that scientists have discovered how certain fish can make themselves magically disappear in the open ocean where there are very few places to hide from sharks and other big and hungry enemies. These fish "hide in the light" by using their silver skin as camouflage to blend in with light waves.

Actually I don't understand how this could happen but I do find the idea interesting. And I love that there are fish who have their own "cape of invisibility" like the superheroes in the comics. And it's fun that they even have appropriate-sounding names—the "big-eyed scad" and the "lookdown."

Some seniors would sure like to have that invisibility cape to hide under when they are having a bad day, stumbling around, trying to keep from tripping over their cane, or looking "big-eyed" when they feel others are looking down on them just because they don't fluently speak the language of computerism.

Lord, how deep the ocean, how high the sky! You made so many kinds of fish and other things that live in the open ocean that is so deep we can't even see the bottom. That reminds me of my refrigerator. Some days it gets so crowded with scads of little leftovers I can't see what strange organisms are hiding in the bottom. My friends would really "lookdown" on me if they saw how disorganized I am. So I"d better start cleaning and stop reading headlines.

Again, Lord, my thanks to you, who are so much greater than all the fish in the sea.

Eyes closed

Dear Lord, this morning I am doing my daily serious reading—the comics page or what we used to call "the funnies." One of them has a grandpa in it, and his little grandson is saying, "My grandpa is so good at taking naps, he can do it with his eyes closed."

There used to be lots of little chores that were so easy to get done that we seniors could "do it with our eyes closed." We can still do a lot of those little things, but our grandkids probably think that the only one we can do easily is take a nap.

Some "surveys" say today that if you have a stressful job, you should stop midday and put your feet up and take a little nap and you will be refreshed for the rest of the day. Most seniors may feel sure that, no matter what a survey says, if they had stopped their job to take a nap in the middle of the day, they might have gotten fired. And that would be even more stressful.

Today, lots of people "work at home," communicating with each other "online." So I guess they really could take little catnaps when needed. Only the computer would know!

Lots of seniors still work at home. They just don't get paid for it.

Cooking, cleaning, writing checks to pay the bills, maybe mowing the lawn or trimming the bushes or walking all the way out in the yard to get the mail or pick up the daily newspaper—those are all necessary jobs, but you should not try them with your eyes closed.

Well, Lord, I have whiled away a bit of this morning reading and chuckling, and I think it has done me more good than taking a nap. But since I am one who works at home, I'd better start working.

Lord, thank you for one of the "rights" of seniority—I can still take a nap or enjoy a chuckle whenever I choose "with my eyes closed."

Good enuff?

Dear Lord, a friend told me she had a doctor's appointment this morning, so I called this afternoon to see how it went. She said, "The doctor said I was good—but not 'good enuff.'"

Oh no! How many times through the years have we heard that phrase—"not good enuff!"

You applied for a job and thought you had a good resume or qualifications. But it was "not good enuff." Somebody with more experience got the job.

You planned a special dinner and used a new recipe and spent a lot of time shopping for the ingredients and cooking them for just the right time. The food turned out good—but "not good enuff" to be special.

You shopped for a new car, household appliance, sofa, TV, or a smarter phone. You were careful and asked other people's advice. You finally made a decision and shelled out your money. It seemed OK at first, but you soon found out it was "not good enuff."

Lord, these are trivial things but I sometimes wonder about more important things. Someone asks us for help, and we maybe give them a little cash or advice or sympathy but then we get busy and never get back to them. Maybe it was "not enuff."

Someone is lonely or sick and wants to talk and you talk. And then, they call again and again. You finally stop answering their calls. Maybe it was "not enuff."

And, Lord, maybe we do the same with prayer. We go on a retreat or day of prayer and we come home filled with passion and piety. We make promises to ourselves to pray more and complain less, but it doesn't last long. Maybe it was "not enuff."

My friend's doctor suggested therapy and a new medicine, and if she follows through with his "prescription," maybe it will eventually be "good enuff!"

Truth be told, as long as we really try to pay attention and be the best we can be, and follow through when it is important, most of our efforts will actually *be* "good enuff."

So, Lord, I pray for my friend today and for all my friends but most of all for me, myself, and I. Help me, Lord, to keep on keeping on. I know I will probably not ever even be good but maybe I can sorta kinda get to be "good enuff."

Tick-tock

Dear Lord, I think I have a clock—big, little, new, old, chiming—in every room of my house. And yes, in the bathroom too. But they all lie to me. I look at a clock, and it tells me it is ten minutes after ten and I need to be somewhere by eleven. The clock says, "Don't worry. You have plenty of time to change clothes, put out the mail, straighten the kitchen, and drive across town." So I "take my time," and then I am dashing and worrying and hurrying, and sometimes I get there at the last minute.

Once I get there and seated, I notice others scurrying in after the last minute, so I know I am not the only one who is living with liar clocks.

Even on Sunday in church, when I should be praying for forgiveness, I look around and see bad-clock people come dashing in at the last minute.

Now that this is on my mind, I remember birthday parties, baby showers, graduations, and even weddings and surprise parties when people arrived at the last minute—or even beyond.

Now, this is one failing I cannot blame on old age. I have had bad clocks since I was a teenager. I have tried throwing out a few clocks and buying new ones but they all tick to the same "last minute illness." Since my clocks are out of control, I guess I will finally, in my senior years, have to confess that I share some of the blame. Now that I am older I can't move as fast as before. No more dashing faster than a speeding bullet. No more leaping deadlines in a single bound. Just limping lamely and lately, like the lollygagger that I truly am.

Sorry, Lord. Do you think that if I set all my clocks fifteen minutes fast I would cherish those last minutes enough to arrive on time?

Maybe I'll try it. But in the meantime, Lord, thank you for all the minutes you give me each day; forgive me for the ones that I waste lollygagging and for the ones I spend wisely if not well. And, Lord, stay by my side, helping me to do your will until that truly last minute.

Peeping Toms

Dear Lord, who's been looking in my window or spying on my personal lifestyle? It's bad enough that my friends and acquaintances can look at me and see that I am growing older (not old-old, you understand, just older). But I am insulted by some people I don't know and have never seen, who live in states where I have never been and never plan to go, people who are complete strangers who know I am growing older without even seeing me. Without ever meeting me, they have my name, address, and probably my choice of tea or coffee. They also seem to know what kind of pains, aches, or ailments I may or may not have.

These are the people who call me on the phone, trying to tell me I need a senior security system, a senior bathtub, a senior magazine, or whatever. These are the people who send me catalogues picturing everything someone who is growing older should need—from canes to crutches to coffee cups with "old" sayings like "I'm not over the hill yet—I'm too tired to climb it."

How did they know? Who gave them my age? And how did they get my medical history?

Well, of course I know it has something to do with a thing once known as a "party line" and is now just "online". And I know some catalogs can be a blessing for seniors who do not drive anymore and have to order things by phone, snail mail, or e-mail. It's just the idea of the loss of privacy.

Dear Lord, I know I am complaining again, busily criticizing the "joys" of today's open-window life, but it's scary to me, realizing that strangers know my phone number, address, and maybe even the numbers on my social security check. They seem to know as much about me as I do myself. Well, maybe more—since I sometimes forget numbers and have to look them up in my trusty book of household "information."

I realize that today people of all ages seem happy to go online and post their most secret thoughts, photos, plans, etc., for all to see; but, Lord, I'd rather share some of that only with you.

Forgive me, Lord, if I gnash my teeth and snarl at the unwelcome callers. It's bad for my teeth and I really should feel sorry for and be patient with people who have to earn a living by irritating senior citizens. Bless them and please help them find a different job.

Artificial friends

Dear Lord, this morning a newspaper headline grabbed my attention: "Artificial Friends for the Aging."

Was this about artificial metal knees or hips, false teeth, hearing aids, or hair dye? No! It was information about how robots and drones may soon be an elder's best friend!

Now that seniors are living longer, inventors are thinking up ways to help us do household chores so we can stay in our homes longer. Who knows when, but in the future, cars will drive themselves to take me to the grocery, small drones will bring me the cane I left in the kitchen or dust the corner or the chandelier, and robots will be my helpers.

Well, this all sounds hopeful—or hopeless. Some seniors will not welcome "artificial friends," and others will be delighted to finally get some help around the house. Already many families are using the magical technology of something named Skype that allows "visits" with family members who live far away by letting them see and talk to each other over their computers. Some families use this for a once-a-week get-together, chatting with friends and loved ones.

This all sounds like make-believe, but it hasn't been too long since people couldn't imagine a microwave oven that could cook dinner in minutes instead of hours.

Any kind of "change" is hard for people of any age, Lord, but without "change" babies wouldn't turn into toddlers and then into teens and adults. And houses wouldn't have indoor plumbing.

So, Lord, help me and all seniors to hold onto our faith and principles, but open our minds to welcome this strange-sounding technology that might someday give us drones and robots and who-knows-what kind of help to do our household chores and live an easier aging life.

While waiting for the changes, Lord, I thank you for making my everyday life always better because I have you to share it with me. You comfort me and inspire me and help me get from one chair to another. Thank you so much.

I've been thinking, Lord, and I think when I get my first robot I will name him Algernon.

Does that sound too fancy? Maybe I will just settle for Sam. Or Bud. Or Nancy. Or maybe artificial or not, the best name would be "Friend."

Helpful herbs?

Dear Lord, a headline I read said, "Have you had your turmeric today?" Sorry to say, I have not. My turmeric is just sitting there in its little bottle on the spice shelf with Basil, Rosemary, and Thyme. I used to try to be a gourmet cook, so I have lots of spices at the ready. I know turmeric is used in many Indian dishes, but I haven't cooked anything that adventurous recently. Now I read that turmeric is good for one's health. It can reduce inflammation and fight arthritis, Alzheimer's disease, and who knows what all else. So maybe I'd better find some turmeric recipes right away. Or maybe not.

I am always reading that this and that will fight that and this, and I want to hurry out to buy and try something new. Sometimes it really helps, and sometimes it doesn't, but then, that's life: great one day, not so much another day. And maybe that's what keeps us young—always trying something new, always seeking.

And speaking of reading and something new, I also read a little thing that might be appropriate for seniors. It's "Lessons learned from a baby." And here are a few: "It's OK to need help to stand on your own two feet…Maybe you just need a change…It's fun to learn something new every day…Laugh a lot…The world is a wonderful place but it *can* get scary…Sometimes all you need is a hug."

I've really got to meditate on those lessons. With all the crazy changes age has brought, I can't help but laugh a lot at myself, and the world *can* be scary when you need help to stand on your own two feet; but whatever happens, all is well when you get that hug. Oh, and there's one more baby lesson, which is my favorite: "People may laugh when you put your foot into your mouth."

Oh, Lord, it is so cute watching a baby chewing on his little piggy toes but not so cute when you are a senior who can barely reach to put her toes into a stocking. Lord, you are well aware of how many times I have put my foot into my mouth. And it isn't easy removing a senior foot gracefully. But that's OK. I know you will help me—the way you always help me to get out of tight situations. And besides, I like to give my friends a foot-in-the-mouth laugh now and then.

Sing-alongs

Dear Lord, yesterday was a balmy day and I was feeling a bit balmy too, so I got a book and drove down to the little lake near our subdivision. I got out and sat on a bench trying to drink in the sunshine. Then I heard some giggly, happy voices coming from a bunch of little girls, maybe a school group or scouts or whatever, but they were singing familiar tunes with different words. I listened as they sang "Row, row, row your boat" but turned it into "Throw, throw, throw your goat." "Take Me Out to the Ballgame" had changed to "Take me Out of School Early'" and "Yankee Doodle Dandy" was "Cranky Noodle Candy." I was surprised they even knew the tune of "Good King Wenceslaus," but they had changed it to "Good King, pass the slaw."

Well, the girls dashed away and I was so happy that I had been at the right place and the right time to hear just what I needed that day. As I giggled and smiled to myself, I decided to make a song for senior citizens, turning "Twinkle, Twinkle, Little Star" into "Wrinkle, wrinkle, where you are."

Lord, you are so good at sending me to places

where I need to be. It isn't always this much fun, but it's always what I need. Sometimes I see someone who looks like she or he has just totally dried up inside and lost the way to find joy. It reminds me to pray for all people like that, senior or not. Or, like today, thanks for reminding me to pray for the youth who are faced with so much ugliness in today's world. Help them see instead all the beauty so they can keep singing and giggling and hopefully helping their friends and family to appreciate your many blessings.

For now, Lord, I'd better get off this bench and get home to string the beans and mash the potatoes before passersby start to wonder what that balmy old lady is doing, just sitting there wrinkling and smiling.

Who was I?

Dear Lord, "The older I get, the more I was." When I read that headline, it really got to me. Older golfers may misremember a few of their past amazing scores in their days of greens. Still-attractive ladies may embroider the romantic portrait of how they once were belles, charming all with their beauty. Successful business people may remember themselves as lions of industry.

Until recently, some older politicians could brag about all the wonderful things they had done to change the world, but today you can google them and find out that some of that "was" is only in his or her "revised" memory.

Of course, none of my friends would be guilty of such dastardly bragging. They are old, and they know it, and they have changed, and they will share the "is" rather than a lot of the "was" with you. Actually, I am the only one of us who *might* sometimes be guilty of making variations, alterations, modifications, amendments, enrichments, and humor when telling some of my crazy stories—of both then and now!

Oh well, Lord, I really enjoyed most of my

"was." I shouldn't talk about it because a lot of my friends were there when it happened, so they already know about it. And my newer friends want to talk more about what is happening now rather than then. And when I start to remember the really "special" times—both the bad and the good—I talk to myself and to you, Lord. You are the only one I want to share those memories with.

So thank you again, Lord, for all the adventures that truly happened and for the ones that may be on the way. Just last week there was some new drama in my life! I had promised to attend a luncheon, picking up a friend on the way there. The night before, I bit into a piece of lettuce (!) and broke off a piece of my front tooth. What to do? What to do? Go to lunch and eat soup? Don't go to lunch and disappoint my friend who needed a ride?

Bright and early in the morning I called my wonder-working dentist and luckily got a nine o'clock appointment. He fixed the tooth in plenty of time for me to keep my lunch appointment.

Thank you, Lord, that drama does not appear every day, but it can sure liven up this old life when a day starts with a bad shock but then has a happy ending.

Footprints

Dear Lord, this morning all was bright and sunny, but it had snowed in the night and decorated the bushes and left what looked like a white tablecloth on my patio floor. I was reminded once again that I do truly have "friends in high places" and today those friends were perched in the high branches of the trees, seated all along the top of the fence; and a few little ones were even on the edge of the snowy bird bath. There was the bright red cardinal, the blue jay, the mockingbird, the robins, the little yellow bird that looks like a canary but isn't, and some unknown birds of a feather. They were waiting for me to throw out some food on that tablecloth.

After I did, they jumped into the snow and feasted. After they flew off to wherever they go off to, I noticed they had left in the snow lots of tiny footprints interweaved into a patio portrait! It was beautiful. But those footprints looked so tiny, and I suddenly wondered if birds have cold feet. Do I need to knit socks?

Lord, if birds need socks, they are in big trouble. My feet are always cold, so I worry about things like that. But I actually tried making socks once and learned that knit is "knot" my thing. Well, Lord, I'm glad you fixed it so that the birds don't need socks, and I thank you for taking care of all of us in so many different ways.

Lord, sometimes I forget to put bird food out on time and I feel so guilty when I look out and see the birds patiently waiting. Give me patience too, Lord. Help me remember to do the things I should do when I should do them. And thank you for decorating my days with so many little surprises like the patio portrait made by bird footprints. And help me keep on keeping on so I won't have to ask for help from "friends in high places" other than the ones in my backyard—and you.

Fast thinking

Dear Lord, I ran into an old friend today. Now why would I say that? I didn't hit her with a car or anything. We just happened to be at the same place at the same time, so it was a happy run-into. We took time to visit over a cup of coffee, and she reminded me of things I had totally forgotten. When we first became friends, we were young, single business women living in the same apartment building, so we often did things together. She reminded me of the little get-togethers I would have at my apartment with a bunch of my advertising friends—people who were used to playing with words. And we played a game where we would turn on the TV but leave the sound off, and then we would "put words in the mouths of the people on TV." At that time we were a fast-thinking, fast-talking bunch, so you would have to call out your words fast before somebody else said something funnier than you could.

It was so long ago, I hardly remember the game, but I do remember the laughs at our get-togethers. Maybe people today still play that game. Oh, not people that I know today. We have become too slow on the draw for that, but it sounds like fun. So, just to test it out, I tried watching TV with the sound off today. There was nobody here to try to get a word in before I did, so I got in a few chuckles all by myself—only because I had no competition. Maybe I'll suggest this game at the next ladies day at my house. But I'd better give them a really good lunch first.

Dear Lord, if I try this game again, maybe I should really talk *to* the people on TV, saying things like, "Why is your music so loud and the words so ugly?" or "Why do so many programs just have explosions, vampires, shootouts, and 'evil doings'?" or "Why do even 'family' shows sometimes include 'dirty' jokes or adult scenes?" And "Why do you twist and tarnish young minds by showing questionable programs at a time when children will be watching?"

Well, Lord, thanks for the "fun" memories, but maybe it's good that when I get steamed up, I only talk to you. Otherwise, my blood pressure might blow a fuse on that bad old TV.

Messages by mail

Dear Lord, when the postman comes, he doesn't ring twice like in the old movie. He just stuffs my box with more catalogs than I can carry. Well, today I decided to look through some, and I find that the catalogs selling T-shirts are the best ones to read.

There is a smart message on so many of the shirts that I could just buy an assortment of shirts for every day in the week and each day just wear the one that seems appropriate for my mood that day.

I'll get the green shirt that has the message: "OOPS...Did I roll my eyes out loud?"

When you are a senior citizen, you may have need to roll your eyes every time you turn on the TV, listen to the radio, meet a teenager, or hear a political speech.

Then I can get the blue T-shirt that simply says, "Finish what you start." I have trouble with that every day. I start sorting the laundry, but the phone rings and I stop to chit-chat. I start to address two birthday cards, but I suddenly remember that I was supposed to pick up a dessert for tonight's potluck, and I head out to the store. I start to make a grocery list but remember I'd better get those birthday cards in the mail.

The pink shirt looks dainty and innocent but the message on it is "'Though she be but little she is fierce.' Shakespeare." I like that one.

And then there's the purple one that hits too close to home. In small but fancy type it reads "I enjoy long romantic walks—to the fridge."

Well, Lord, it's pitiful when your life story is there for all to see on a bunch of T-shirts. Maybe I should try to get a shirt made with the message "I'll try to do better tomorrow."

Second chances

Dear Lord, this morning a friend who has been desperately looking for a new job called to tell me good news. A couple weeks ago, she interviewed for a job she really wanted—but didn't get. She has been so worried; but yesterday she applied for a different job that was even better than the one she didn't get—and she got it! We both suddenly said, "When a door closes, God opens a window."

After we hung up, I began remembering the many times in my life when I got a "second chance." The first one changed my life. I had a job I loved, writing radio and TV commercials for a small advertising company in my hometown. I had met a man I thought was Mr. Right, and we were talking about getting married; so life was good. Then we broke up because of a little tiff about something trivial, and he moved away to a new job in another town. While I was still recovering from that, I learned that my "perfect" job might end soon since the company was in dire financial trouble. And then, out of the blue, I was offered a bigger job with a bigger paycheck from a bigger, nationally known company where I had interviewed months before.

There was one problem. I would have to move away to a new town where I knew no one and would be totally on my own. Probably because of my earlier disappointment, I felt brave enough to do that. And that's where I found the man who really was Mr. Right, and I learned to enjoy being a housewife and mother and even found time to start writing books instead of ads.

Dear Lord, how many times you have generously given me a "second chance." Thank you so much. Now that I have lived so long, I can look back and rejoice that so many closed doors led to new and wonderful windows.

I pray today, Lord, for those who may be looking at closed doors—that they will have the faith to wait for you to help them find a ray of sunshine coming through an open window. And, Lord, help them have the courage to recognize and take the "second chance" when it comes—and follow it, with you at their side.

And the winner is...

Dear Lord, my niece sent me the funniest birthday card I received this year. It has a picture on the front of a cute little girl, about five years old, dressed in a fancy, little-girl dress, with a sparkly, glittery crown on her head. She is smiling and waving, obviously pleased to be the winner of a little-girl beauty pageant. Inside, the card's message reads, "Let's not say you are getting older, let's just say your pageant days are numbered!"

It was a good giggle for the day—but it made me sad too.

Actually my pageant days were numbered a long time ago. I was never pageant material, and my mother would have never wanted me to be in one, but she did like to "pretty me up." Looking at old photographs, I can see that when I was about five years old, my mother tortured my hair into Shirley Temple curls, hand-made my "go to church" dresses with lots of ruffles and frou-frou, and always crowned me by putting a huge bow of ribbon on the top of my head. Back in the day, maybe bows were "in" and maybe that's why, in the photos, my mother and I are both smiling as brightly as the pageant princess on my birthday card.

Through the years I managed to recover from the fear of frou-frou and hair bows, but today anything and everything seems to be in fashion; and sadly, pageants are shockingly different from yesteryear—even little girl pageants. Now mothers "decorate" their little girls with lipstick and mascara and special hairdos and teach them inappropriate songs and dances. And the older girls in the beauty pageants wear almost-there bathing suits and gowns. But maybe their days are numbered too. Maybe we will get back to a simpler, innocent time one of these days.

Dear Lord, with all the children, teens, and adults glued to their "machines" today, easily finding ways to read and "learn" things way beyond their years and understanding, it will be hard to ever go back, but we must pray for that. Please help today's generations—children, teens, young, and old—to look and appreciate and rejoice in all the "good" things you have put into our lives.

Joy jars?

Dear Lord, I remember not too many years ago when many homes had a "job jar." It was usually in the kitchen, sitting next to a little pad of paper and a pencil. Whenever there were little family jobs to be done, somebody (usually mom) would write down the chore on a little piece of paper and put it in the jar. Then when someone had a few free minutes, they would pull out a piece of paper and see what "to-do" was needed. There would be small and large jobs—like water the plants, trim the shrubs, wash out the garbage cans, fold the laundry, wash the dog, or clean the cat's water bowl.

I doubt anyone still has a job jar, but recently someone gave me something similar—a cute little flower-trimmed jar that was labelled "Blessings." You are supposed to write on little pieces of paper the names of blessings and put those in the jar. You might write, "friends," "hope," "laughter," "warm bed," "fun," "support," faith," "love," "family," "health," "joy," "growth," based on whatever is going on in your senior life. Then when you are having a *mizzable*, challenging, or lonely day, you can take out one of the papers and think about it and pray about it and maybe even have a chuckle about how blessed you really are.

Dear Lord, often it can be the "little things" that make our days. The news reports huge problems, wars, and rumors of wars on the other side of the world, people suffering, people sinning in terrible ways, tornadoes, floods, drug problems, shootings. And what can seniors do about any or all of it but pray and hope? Well, I'm gonna fill my little jar today, and I will be prepared when the next *mizzable* day comes along.

Inspiration and desperation

Dear Lord, many of my friends keep up with the news, read big educational books, see the best movies, and know how to use the Internet. Good for them. I am so grateful they can pass on their knowledge to me when I need it. And I need it because recently I get my inspiration from signs advertised in catalogs, paperback, easy-to-read books, and pithy thoughts wherever I can find them. For example, I found a bit of advice that suggested, "Gratitude turns what we have into Enough." Oh, how soon I learned that when my husband and I were newlyweds with one car, a small house, one baby, and just enough money to be enough. And it was fun.

Now that I am a senior, I like the advice "Until God opens the next door, praise him in the hallway." Ah, I do praise you, Lord—in the hallway, the basement, the patio, the front yard, the garage and my favorite burger barn. On a birthday card I saw "Count your blessings, not your birthdays." That one is easy, since I was never very good at math. And then there is the wise old saying: "Lord, keep your arm around my shoulder and your hand over my mouth."

Lord, with all this inspiration, in spite of my desperation, you keep giving me more wonderful happenings, adventures, friends, and blessings. Thank you.

Cold feet

Dear Lord, while working one of my ever-ready crossword puzzles today, I discovered an amazing bit of trivia. I learned that the big toe on the Statue of Liberty is six feet long! I was particularly interested in this because one of my big toes feels like it is six feet long and it is *angry*. It started a while back when that toe hurt if I wore a certain shoe, so I switched to a different pair of shoes... and another and another. Finally, I only had one pair of shoes that this toe could feel comfy walking around in.

I let it go too long because so many of my friends have *big* problems—hip replacements, various kinds of operations or serious illnesses. When they were telling me of their "ails," I did not feel comfortable to say, "My big toe hurts." But finally I went to a foot doctor and he worked on it and found something hiding under the nail; and then my big toe even got x-rayed. You would think that would make a good impression on the toe, but it still does not really like most of my shoes.

Oh well, now that I know Lady Liberty has a six-foot-long big toe and no warm, comfy shoes,

I feel a strange kind of connection with her. She has a hard job holding up that torch all the time, welcoming the tired, the poor, the yearning to be free while standing in the whirling winds that blow around her, probably giving her cold feet. But with all the sadness and badness, the goodness and gladness, that whirl around our world today, Liberty, the symbol of freedom, would probably also be hesitant to say "My big toe hurts."

Dear Lord, thank you that I never get "cold feet," feeling afraid to talk to you about everything— even my bothersome big toe.

To dry or not to dry

Dear Lord, yesterday I was having a rare clean-up, wash-up day, so I went to the basement and loaded up some laundry. The first load came out of the dryer all warm and clean and unwrinkled as it should. When I put the next batch in to dry, my quiet little hummer of a dryer suddenly sounded like a metal-on-metal three-car pileup on the highway. I turned it off and went upstairs and had a nice warm cup of coffee and a case of the heebie-jeebies. The handyman who used to fix anything that went bad in this house is no longer available so I had to go to Plan B.

Hoping for help, I called a couple of friends, but they said they didn't have a helper either so if I found one to give them his number. Time for Plan C. As I have mentioned before, Lord, I have days when it is necessary to "furniture walk," so yesterday it was time for "furniture dry" day. Luckily, most of the undried batch was winter wash-n-wear slacks that had come out of the washer damp instead of dripping wet, so I draped them over the kitchen chairs, the rocking chair or anywhere I could find to drape. I kept turning them around to dry the other side, and by the end of the day they were all ready to be hung in the closet. Then the word closet reminded me that my "helpful" son has been urging me to get a smaller washer/dryer set installed in an upstairs closet so I would not be in danger of falling and breaking something when I go down the basement stairs.

Now, instead of just finding a handyman, I will need to get rid of the old dryer, shop for appliances that will fit in a closet, find a very handy man who will know how to hook them up, and then, worst of all, I will have to clear out a closet.

As you see, Lord, it is dangerous to have a clean-up, wash-up day. Since I will now be very busy, you may not hear much from me for a while. Or you may hear from me more than ever, asking for help, not just for the work and worry of getting the job done but also asking forgiveness for the big black cloud of irritation that will probably hang steadily over my head as I complain about another "change" in my senior life.

Think again!

Dear Lord, when I was having coffee with a neighbor this morning, she was looking more "down" than usual, so I asked what was wrong. She said she was thinking she must be really getting old because she was forgetting "little things" she should remember. Then she said, "Did you ever 'stop to think' and then forget to start again?"

Did I ever! I will be making one of my ever-necessary lists and stop to think what to add next when the phone rings and I stop to chat and forget to "start again" on the list. Then I will get to the grocery and reach in my purse for the list—which I left at home on the kitchen table.

But this is one thing I cannot blame on "getting older." This is something I have been doing ever since I became a young housewife and learned how many "little things" I need to take care of every day—things that might not get done unless I have a list to help me remember them. I don't know if this reassured my friend or just made her start to look for younger friends, but I tried.

Dear Lord, as my life has changed, so have my lists, but now I have learned to leave my car keys on the kitchen table so I can't leave home without a list. And when I "stop to think" of whatever old-age problems are bothering me each day, I try to not make a list of them but remember and rejoice in all the good things that remind me to tell you "Thanks!"

Get over it!

Dear Lord, why is it that so many think it is sad and bad to be a senior citizen? What are they thinking? It can be great to be a senior! OK, some days, your back hurts or you are distressed by all the bad news around the world or you can't drive anymore or you have trouble walking or hearing or reaching or socializing. So what? Get over it.

It's all a matter of faith, hope, and charity. Have faith that God is your friend. Hope that something interesting will happen tomorrow—and it probably will. And be charitable to others, realizing they have troubles too.

Everybody always wants to be happy, so after doing intensive (!) research, here are my answers to how to be a happy senior.

Remember that a bad attitude is like a flat tire. Until you change it you are not going anywhere.

Choose to be happy. Whatever happens, see the bright side, *not* the woe-is-me side.

Take pride in whatever you can achieve, no matter how trivial.

Unless the weather is frightful, try to get outside for just a few minutes every day. A bit of fresh air and maybe some sunshine can help you step away from whatever is bothering you.

Remember that no matter how positive you are, there is always someone who can suck the air right out of your red balloon. So just smile, try to act "impressed," and then pray for that person.

Always take time for fun. Read the "funny papers" if you still have a newspaper that includes them. Watch a funny program on TV. Look in a mirror and make funny faces at yourself. Eat ice cream. Or maybe a cookie or two. And if your diet doesn't allow sweets, eat a pickle and work very hard to pretend it is a candy bar.

Lord, I don't know if any of my "research" will work for anybody else, but it works for me. I *am* a happy senior. And I thank you so much for all the memories, all the years in the past and in the present. And I can't wait to see what joy, what fun, what miracle may be waiting around the next corner.